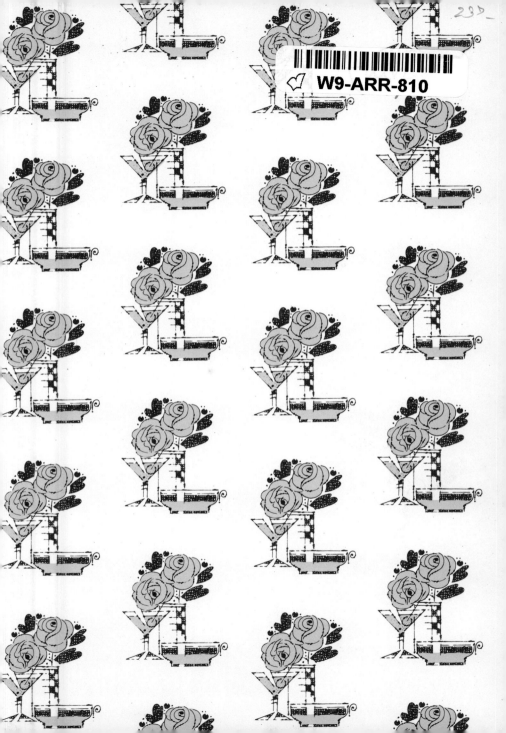

THE
JEEVES
GUIDE TO
MIXED
DRINKING

THE JEEVES COCKTAIL BOOK

A GUIDE TO MIXED DRINKING

Ebury Press

Anita M.

Illustrations:
RUSSELL COULSON

Dialogue:
HUGH BREDIN
(with acknowledgements to and in admiration of P. G. Wodehouse)

Special consultant:
ROGER METCALFE
President, United Kingdom Bartenders' Guild

Planned and produced by:
Tigerlily Limited
34 Marshall Street, London W1

PUBLISHED BY EBURY PRESS
National Magazine House
72 Broadwick Street, London W1V 2BP

First impression 1980

ISBN 085223 176 8

Filmset in Great Britain by
BAS Printers Limited, Over Wallop, Hampshire
and bound by G & J Kitcat Limited, London

CONTENTS

INTRODUCTION

Jeeves is noted for his tissue-restorers. The morning after Boat Race night or a toot at the Drones Club, I have sometimes dreamed that some bounder was driving spikes through my head. At such times I reach out a hand shaking like an aspen and ring for Jeeves. He shimmers out and, almost instanter, returns with a bracer from the icebox. I loose it down the Wooster hatch and, after undergoing the passing discomfort of having the skull fly up to the ceiling and the eyes shoot out of their sockets and rebound from the opposite wall, like racquets balls, I feel better. Still, after partaking of one of these morning mixtures, the patient is well advised not to oscillate the bean for an hour or so.

But here I go, dash it! I am already drifting from the nub or crux: to wit, the cocktail in every shape and form. Jeeves, as in all else, is an expert in these matters. Ask him for something traditional such as a Manhattan, a Screwdriver, a Prairie Oyster or a Sidecar, and he will procure the definitive version of same: dematerializing like one of those fellows in India—fakirs, I think they're called—only to turn up seconds later at your elbow, all parts reassembled, with a brimming stoup of the ordered fluid.

Again, when some soul in torment, deep in the mulligatawny and with no hope of striking for the shore, hoves to and drops despondent anchor at the Wooster residence, the hour will find the man and the man the drink. Jeeves will call on his creative juices—his, Jeeves's that is, not the bimbo immersed in the bouillon—and deliver a brew expressly suited to the circs. Which brings me to the matter of Jeeves, Bertram Wooster and little differences between us.

When two men of iron share a roof there is bound to be the odd rift within the lute, and mixed drinks are no exception. Several racy concoctions have prompted Jeeves to use the old eyebrow routine. Some of these were created by yours truly, others by various members of the Drones, notably Catsmeat Potter-Pirbright who, if he didn't draw his weekly envelope treading the boards in London's better-known theatres, could make his pile by agitating a cocktail-shaker in any prime night-spot in London, New York or points west.

In fact, it was Catsmeat who introduced me to the Acapulco Sunset, an unparalleled mélange of rum, brandy, beaujolais, bitters and much else besides. At the time, I was staying at Brinkley Court, Worcs, home of my good

8

and deserving Aunt Dahlia, employer of the chef, Anatole, a hash-slinger without peer. I was slated at no distant date to don the spongebag trousers and gardenia and walk up the aisle with Madeline. Fearful that, with nuptials in the offing, I would find myself but toying with Anatole's Selle d'Agneau à la Greque, I drank deep of the flowing bowl produced by Catsmeat.

Serenity and a sense of *bien-être* were instantly restored. Thanks to the Potter-Pirbright tonic, I shovelled the unbeatable eatables into myself like a stevedore slipping a grain ship its mid-morning rations.

But when, on another occasion, I asked Jeeves to slip self and other guests an Acapulco Sunset, he delivered a firm *nolle prosequi* and returned from his lair with beakers of whisky and soda. A decent enough snootful, I grant you, but not the rainbow-hued item on the agenda.

This is not to demean the scope of Jeeves's recipes for cocktails as laid down in this slim volume. Every one of them is a humdinger, tried and tested by the members of Jeeves's club, the Junior Ganymede, that meeting place of the crème de la crème of gentlemen's personal gentlemen, butlers and, Jeeves tells me, the occasional footman. And every mixed drink in this book, I may tell you, is absolutely AO-bally-K by the Wooster palate, too. 'Let's call it *Stirring Times with Wooster Sauces*, Jeeves,' I said when this project was first mooted, not a little proud of so apt an exhibition of word-play.

'I would suggest, sir, that such a title be ill-advised in the present case,' he averred, with a certain what-is-it in his voice—*froideur*, perhaps? 'With respect, your public expect something with a little more *gravitas*.'

'*Gravitas*, Jeeves?'

'The Latin, sir, for weight, carrying the implication of seriousness and possibly scholarship accrued over many years of correctly interpreted experience. Might I put forward for your consideration *The Jeeves Cocktail Book—A Guide to Mixed Drinking?*'

I inclined the bean, and considered. As so often before, the chances were that the fellow had something.

Bertie Wooster

THE FIXINGS

We Woosters are never slow to give credit where it's due. No one living can come across with a snifter that's a patch on Jeeves's line in mixed drinks. I have acquired all my knowledge in the field from the fellow. What better way, I once thought when Jeeves was going off for his annual holiday, to bring the blue bird out of the hat in his absence, than to persuade him to let me in on a few tricks of the trade.

'Jeeves, before you take off to Herne Bay for the shrimping, will you give me the lowdown on the finer points of throwing together brews suited to the cocktail hour?'

'I am deeply flattered, sir, and will proceed to do so with great pleasure.'

With that, Jeeves conducted me to his lair and, with appropriate gestures, named the equipment you see below.

'I've absorbed all that, Jeeves. But what of measures?'

'In the recipes here, sir, you will see that most of the ingredients are given in proportions. The size of glass will dictate whether the drink is long or short. But I have also taken the liberty of using a measure, sir. A measure is a definite quantity. Exactly a third of a gill, or approximately one jigger, $1\frac{1}{2}$ fluid ounces, or two tablespoons.'

'Two tablespoonfuls for me, Jeeves. Other customers may opt as may be.'

'Very good, sir. Now for the cocktail shaker. One places ice in, thus; pours in the necessary ingredients and then shakes the implement with a brisk, sharp motion before straining into the recommended glass.'

'Straining, Jeeves?'

'Yes, sir. It prevents ice from invading the cocktail when it is poured from shaker or mixing glass to the drinking glass.'

'Just like tea, Jeeves, what?'

'Precisely, sir. As for mixing glasses, one places the ice in first, then the

Cocktail Cabinet Equipment:

Cocktail Shaker   Mixing glass

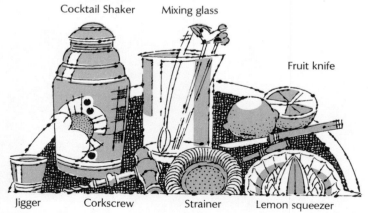

Fruit knife

Jigger   Corkscrew   Strainer   Lemon squeezer

necessary ingredients. Next one stirs until cold before straining into the drinking glass.'

'Any inside info on ice, Jeeves?'

'To crush it, sir, one wraps some cubes in a clean cloth and knocks them forcefully against a hard surface or hits them with a blunt instrument.'

'Like a guardian of the peace putting it across the evil-doer?'

'Or vice-versa, sir.'

'And what of "twist", Jeeves?'

'That refers to the peel of orange or lemon, sir. When a recipe includes a "twist", the peel should first be squeezed above the surface of the drink to release the oil it contains, then the peel may be dropped into the glass.'

'Some recipes refer to sugar syrup, Jeeves. What steps does the man of the world take to produce that?'

'One takes a pint of water, sir, a pound of sugar in cube or granulated form, and one teaspoon of glucose. One then places these ingredients in a pan and boils them on a high heat for about two minutes. If any froth appears on the surface, one removes it with a spoon. It is then essential, sir, to put the sugar syrup in an airtight container and store it somewhere cool.'

'Like a refrigerator, Jeeves?'

'That would serve extremely well, sir'.

'Well, Jeeves, while you are netting choice specimens of seafood on your holiday, you can imagine me, when the sun's over the yardarm, following your instructions to the final drop. And that done, retiring to an armchair to put the feet up, sipping with carefree content, rather like Caesar having one in his tent the day he overcame the Nervii.'

'I shall take great pleasure in conjuring up the vision you suggest, sir.'

Glasses: Tall Champagne glass   Wine glass (goblet)   Highball glass
(approx 8 oz)   (approx 8 oz)   (10 oz)

Old Fashioned glass
(approx 8 oz)

Cocktail glass   Beer mug or tankard   Punchbowl and cups.
(approx $3\frac{1}{2}$ oz)   (1 pint or $\frac{1}{2}$ pint)

A FEW QUICK ONES

'Well, Jeeves, what news on the Rialto?'

'Miss Honoria Glossop telephoned to say that she and her father, Sir Roderick, were paying you a visit at noon today, sir. It would appear that her engagement to Mr. Biffen has been sundered.'

The statement smote me like a ton of bricks. I shot Jeeves a significant glance. He knows just how matters stand with H. Glossop and self, but the Woosters and the Jeeveses never bandy a lady's name.

Honoria had once attempted to mould the Wooster soul preparatory to matrimony. When the clay disintegrated into sand and slipped through her fingers, she had turned her attentions to Biffy Biffen, but had indicated that, should she have cause to revise her conviction that he was a king among men, Bertram was next in line.

'What am I to do, Jeeves? Steps must be taken.'

'It would certainly seem advisable, sir. May I suggest you play the role of what the French call the *raisonneur*?'

'You mean have a bash at seeing what a calm, kindly man of the world can say to Honoria to bring the young couple together?'

'Precisely, sir. And may I suggest a Dry Martini? I surmise that the potation would enable you to express yourself with even more dexterity and force than you usually bring to your colloquies with Miss Honoria and her father.'

I eyed him reverently. He flickered for an instant and was gone about the business of salvaging the Wooster bacon.

BOODLE'S COCKTAIL

$\frac{1}{3}$ gin

$\frac{1}{3}$ sweet vermouth

$\frac{1}{3}$ fresh orange juice

Shake and strain into a cocktail glass.

BOODLE'S ORIGINAL

$\frac{1}{4}$ gin

$\frac{1}{4}$ Cointreau

$\frac{1}{4}$ dry vermouth

$\frac{1}{4}$ fresh orange juice

Shake and strain into a cocktail glass.

DAIQUIRI

$\frac{3}{4}$ white rum

$\frac{1}{4}$ fresh lime or lemon juice

Few dashes of sugar syrup

Shake and strain into a cocktail glass.

DRY MARTINI

1 measure gin

Few dashes of dry vermouth

Twist of lemon peel

Olive (optional)

Stir and strain into a cocktail glass or serve 'on the rocks'.
Add lemon peel.

ET TU BRUTE

$\frac{1}{2}$ vodka

$\frac{1}{4}$ dry vermouth

$\frac{1}{4}$ crème de cassis

Stir with ice in a wine glass.

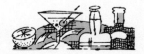

GIBSON

1 measure gin
Few dashes of dry vermouth
Cocktail onion

Stir and strain into a cocktail glass.

GIMLET

$\frac{4}{5}$ gin
$\frac{1}{5}$ fresh lime juice
Dash of soda water (optional)

Stir and strain into a cocktail glass.

GIN AND FRENCH

$\frac{3}{4}$ gin
$\frac{1}{4}$ dry vermouth
Twist of lemon peel
Olive (optional)

Stir and strain into a cocktail glass.
Squeeze lemon peel over drink and drop into glass.
Add olive, if required.

GIN AND IT

$\frac{1}{2}$ gin
$\frac{1}{2}$ sweet vermouth
Maraschino cherry

Stir in a cocktail glass with ice. Add cherry.

GIN FIZZ

| 1 measure gin |
| Juice of one lemon |
| 1 teaspoon of sugar |
| Soda water to top up |

Shake and strain into a wine glass. Top up with soda water.

GIN RICKEY

| Juice and rind of one lime (or lemon) |
| 2 measures gin (whisky, rum or brandy can be used) |
| Soda water to top up |

Extract juice from the lime (or lemon) and put it in an old-fashioned glass along with the rind and some ice. Add spirit, stir and top up with soda water.

GIN SLING

| 1 teaspoon of sugar |
| 1 measure gin (whisky, rum or brandy) |
| Juice of one lemon |
| Slice of lemon |

Dissolve sugar in a little water in a highball glass.
Add spirit, lemon juice and ice and top up with water.
Stir. Decorate with slice of lemon.

HARVEY WALLBANGER

| $\frac{1}{3}$ vodka |
| $\frac{2}{3}$ fresh orange juice |
| Galliano |

Stir vodka and orange juice with ice in a highball glass.
Float two teaspoons of Galliano on top. Serve with straws.

JAMAICA RUM

$\frac{4}{5}$ dark rum

$\frac{1}{5}$ sugar syrup

Dash of Angostura bitters

Stir and strain into a cocktail glass.

JEZEBEL

$\frac{1}{2}$ red wine

$\frac{1}{2}$ fresh orange juice

Shake and pour into a wine glass over crushed ice.
Serve with short straws.

KIR

Chilled dry white wine

Dash of crème de cassis

Twist of lemon peel

Fill wine glass with white wine, add dash of cassis and the lemon peel.

MACARONI

$\frac{2}{3}$ pastis

$\frac{1}{3}$ sweet vermouth

Shake and strain into a cocktail glass.

MANHATTAN

$\frac{2}{3}$ rye

$\frac{1}{3}$ sweet (or dry) vermouth

Dash of Angostura bitters

Maraschino cherry (or twist of lemon peel for the dry version)

Stir and strain into a cocktail glass.

NEGRONI

$\frac{1}{3}$ gin

$\frac{1}{3}$ sweet vermouth

$\frac{1}{3}$ Campari

Soda water to top up (optional)

Half slice of orange

Pour over ice in an old-fashioned glass.
Top up with soda water if desired and add the slice of orange.

OH HENRY

$\frac{1}{4}$ Scotch

$\frac{1}{4}$ B and B

$\frac{1}{2}$ Seven Up

Serve on the rocks in a wine glass.

SCREWDRIVER

$\frac{1}{3}$ vodka

$\frac{2}{3}$ fresh orange juice

Stir in a wine glass with ice.

SHERRY COCKTAIL

2 oz medium dry sherry

$\frac{1}{4}$ oz dry vermouth

4 dashes of orange bitters

Stir well and strain into a cocktail glass.

SLOE GIN

$\frac{1}{2}$ sloe gin

$\frac{1}{4}$ dry vermouth

$\frac{1}{4}$ sweet vermouth

Stir and strain into a cocktail glass.

TANTALIZER

$\frac{1}{2}$ blue curaçao

$\frac{1}{2}$ anisette

Shake and strain into a cocktail glass.

TOM COLLINS

1 measure gin

Juice of one lemon

1 teaspoon of sugar

Slice of lemon

Soda water to top up

Put ingredients with ice into a highball glass, top up with soda
water and serve with a slice of lemon and straws.

WHISKY SOUR

1 measure bourbon or rye

1 teaspoon of sugar syrup

Juice of one lemon

Few dashes of egg white (optional)

Soda water to top up

Slice of lemon

Shake and strain into a champagne glass, top up with soda water
and add slice of lemon.

COCKTAILS FOR TWO

'Jeeves, it is the maddest, merriest day in all the glad new year.'

'I am gratified to hear you say so, sir.'

'I have decided to take the plunge.'

'Very good, sir. The red and black bathing slip we purchased in Antibes or the navy blue with the discreet yellow stripes?'

'You misunderstand me, Jeeves. I refer to matrimony, not the briny.'

'With Miss Wickham, sir?'

'With Miss Wickham, Jeeves.'

'Well, sir . . .'

'There is nothing to say "Well, sir" about. The hearts of Roberta Wickham and self beat as one. Set up two potions. I have a tryst with Miss Wickham and am poised to plight my troth.'

'Very good sir.'

It was with a forgiving beam that I welcomed him when he returned with the needful. I took a preliminary sip to hoist the Wooster nerve to concert pitch.

Several hours—or was it days—later, I woke. And the first thought that crept into the throbbing lemon was something Jeeves had once said about how, when a wife comes in at the front door, the valet goes out at the back.

'76

½ bourbon

¼ yellow Chartreuse

¼ fresh lime juice

Few dashes of egg white

Maraschino cherries

Shake well and strain into cocktail glasses. Decorate with cherries.

BLACK RUSSIAN

⅔ vodka

⅓ Kahlua

Serve on the rocks in old-fashioned glasses.

BETWEEN THE SHEETS

⅓ brandy

⅓ white rum

⅓ Cointreau

Dash of lemon juice

Shake and strain into cocktail glasses.

BRANDY ALEXANDER

⅓ brandy

⅓ crème de cacao

⅓ cream

Shake and strain into cocktail glasses.

CHAMPAGNE COCKTAIL

Iced champagne

Dash of brandy

Lump sugar

Angostura bitters

Slices of orange

Put a lump of sugar in each champagne glass and saturate with angostura bitters. Add brandy and fill glasses with champagne. Decorate with orange.

GRASSHOPPER

$\frac{1}{3}$ crème de menthe

$\frac{1}{3}$ crème de cacao

$\frac{1}{3}$ cream

Shake and strain into cocktail glasses.

GREEN MONKEY

2 measures Scotch

Few dashes of green Chartreuse

Few dashes of yellow Chartreuse

Stir well and strain into two ice-filled wine glasses.

HAPPY RETURN

2 measures gin

1 measure fresh lemon juice

2 teaspoons cherry brandy

2 teaspoons Cointreau

Shake and strain into two cocktail glasses.

KING GEORGE VI

$\frac{1}{3}$ Scotch

$\frac{1}{3}$ fresh orange juice

$\frac{1}{6}$ fresh lemon juice

$\frac{1}{6}$ apricot brandy

Shake well and strain into wine glasses.

LIFTER

$\frac{1}{3}$ Cointreau

$\frac{1}{3}$ Campari

$\frac{1}{3}$ fresh orange juice

Shake and strain into cocktail glasses.

LEAPER

½ vodka

½ Cointreau

Juice of two oranges

Few dashes of Maraschino

A black grape to decorate each glass

Shake and strain into cocktail glasses.
Suspend grape on a cocktail stick across the top of each glass.

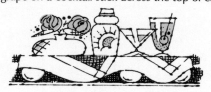

LILLIBET

2 measures gin

Juice of 2 lemons

2 teaspoons sugar

Ginger ale or ginger beer to top up

Shake and strain into two highball glasses.
Top up each glass with the ginger ale or ginger beer.

MANDARINE ROYALE

2 measures mandarine liqueur

½ measure fresh lemon juice

¼ measure sugar syrup

Little white of egg

Champagne to top up

Shake very well and strain into this champagne glasses.
Float champagne on the top.

MARGARITA

2 measures tequila

½ measure fresh lemon juice

¼ measure Cointreau

Salt

Moisten rims of two cocktail glasses with lemon juice and dip rims
in the salt. Shake cocktail and strain into glasses.

OLD FASHIONED

2 measures bourbon or rye
2 lumps of sugar
Few dashes of angostura bitters
Half a slice of orange
Maraschino cherry

Put ingredients with ice in two old-fashioned glasses and stir.
Decorate with orange and cherry.

SCOTCH MIST

2 measures Scotch
Twists of lemon peel

Shake with crushed ice and serve in two old-fashioned glasses
without straining. Add lemon peel and serve with short straws.

SNAKE IN THE GRASS

$\frac{1}{4}$ gin
$\frac{1}{4}$ Cointreau
$\frac{1}{4}$ dry vermouth
$\frac{1}{4}$ fresh lemon juice

Shake and strain into cocktail glasses.

STINGER

$\frac{2}{3}$ brandy
$\frac{1}{3}$ white crème de menthe

Stir and strain into cocktail glasses.

WHITE LADY

$\frac{1}{2}$ gin
$\frac{1}{4}$ Cointreau
$\frac{1}{4}$ fresh lemon juice
Few dashes of egg white

Shake and strain into cocktail glasses.

THE MAESTRO AT MIXING TIME

'Yes, Jeeves?' I said, sluicing a bottle of rum into a tureen already awash with gin, champagne, whisky and a dash of bitters. 'Something on your mind?'

'You are not proposing to serve that mixture to the assembled company, sir?'

'Yes, Jeeves.'

Nobody has a greater respect for Jeeves's intellect than I have, but this disposition of his to dictate to the hand that fed him had, I felt, to be checked. This cocktail—all the rage they'd told me on the Cote d'Azur—would make the party zing.

'It is wholly unsuitable, sir.'

'I do not agree with you, Jeeves. You are hidebound and reactionary in the matter of refreshment. I expect acclaim from all present.' I added five dashes of vinegar, three egg whites and a quart of Calvados. 'No argument, Jeeves, no discussion.'

'Very good, sir.'

I agitated the receptacle, strained it into a serried rank of goblets, topped each with grated nutmeg and gestured to the fellow to pass amongst the guests with the loaded tray.

Pongo Twistleton drained the first glass and ran, clutching his frame, from the room. Boko Fittleworth sipped the second. He beat all records for jumping from a sedentary posture, and chased after Pongo. An aunt followed suit.

'Enough, Jeeves, I concede defeat. Kindly dispose of this mixture and mix a stoup of your Frozen Daiquiri.'

'I have already anticipated your second request, sir. I regret that the first must wait. The bathroom promises to be heavily over-subscribed for some time to come.'

BRANDY SMASH

1 measure brandy (Bacardi rum, gin or whisky)
1 lump of sugar
4 sprigs of mint
Slice of orange, twist of lemon
Mint and a Maraschino cherry to decorate

Dissolve sugar in a little water in an old-fashioned glass, and crush together with the sprigs of mint. Add the spirit and ice and squeeze the lemon over the drink. Decorate with fruit and mint leaves and serve with straws.

CHOP NUT

$\frac{1}{2}$ vodka
$\frac{1}{8}$ crème de banane
$\frac{1}{8}$ orgeat syrup (almond syrup)
$\frac{1}{8}$ cream
$\frac{1}{8}$ fresh orange juice

Shake and strain into a highball glass.

EVERTON BLUE

$\frac{1}{4}$ gin
$\frac{1}{4}$ blue curaçao
$\frac{1}{4}$ crème de banane
$\frac{1}{4}$ cream
Dash of lemon juice
Dash of Grenadine to float on top

Shake all ingredients except Grenadine and strain into a champagne glass. Add dash of Grenadine so that the drink is red at the bottom and blue at the top.

FROZEN DAIQUIRI

1 measure white rum
Juice of one lime (or lemon)
$\frac{1}{2}$ teaspoon of sugar syrup
Dash of Maraschino

Shake with crushed ice and serve unstrained in a wine glass with short straws.

HORSE'S NECK

1 measure brandy
Dash of angostura bitters (optional)
Whole rind of one lemon
Dry ginger ale or soda water to top up

Attach one end of the lemon peel to the rim of a highball glass, allowing the remainder to curl down inside. Anchor the peel with ice. Add the brandy and top up with the ginger ale or soda water.

HONG KONG GIN FIZZ

1 measure gin
$\frac{1}{4}$ measure white rum
$\frac{1}{4}$ measure vodka
$\frac{1}{4}$ measure tequila
$\frac{1}{4}$ measure white curaçao
$\frac{1}{4}$ measure green Chartreuse
$\frac{1}{4}$ measure yellow Chartreuse
1 measure fresh lemon juice

Shake and strain into a highball glass.

MATADOR

$\frac{1}{3}$ tequila
$\frac{1}{3}$ crème de cassis
$\frac{1}{3}$ fresh lemon juice
Sugar to taste

Shake well and strain into a cocktail glass.

MINT JULEP

2 measures bourbon (or rye)
1 tablespoon caster sugar
1 tablespoon water
4 to 6 sprigs of mint

Crush mint, sugar and water with a spoon in a highball glass.
When sugar is dissolved, add bourbon and fill the glass with
crushed ice. Stir until the outside of the glass is frosted. Decorate
with more mint and serve with straws.

SINGAPORE SLING

$\frac{1}{2}$ gin
$\frac{1}{4}$ fresh lemon juice
$\frac{1}{4}$ cherry brandy
Soda water to top up

Shake and strain over more ice in a highball glass.
Top up with soda water.

WHIZZ BANG

$\frac{2}{3}$ Scotch
$\frac{1}{3}$ dry vermouth
2 dashes pastis
2 dashes Grenadine
2 dashes orange bitters

Stir and strain into a cocktail glass.

ZOMBIE

1 measure rum
1 measure dark rum
1 measure white rum
Juice of one lime
Few dashes papaya juice
Few dashes apricot brandy
Few dashes cherry brandy
151° rum to top up
Green and red cherry and slice of orange to decorate

Put crushed ice in a highball glass. Add ingredients and stir. Top up with 151° rum. Decorate with the cherries and a slice of orange. Serve with straws.

UPPER LIP STIFFENERS

'Mrs. Spencer-Gregson is arriving in ten minutes, sir.'

'This is grave news, Jeeves. A world without aunts would be a better world. Don't the Turks shove them in sacks and drop them in the Bosphorus?'

'Odalisques, sir, I understand. Not aunts.'

'Mind you, Jeeves, there are aunts and aunts. But Aunt Agatha is in a class of her own. She chews bottles, wears barbed wire next to the skin and kills rats with her teeth.'

'Indeed, sir'

'Yes, if you're fond of a quiet life, Jeeves, you simply curl into a ball when you see her coming and hope for the best. She has moral suasion down to a fine art.'

'That reminds me, sir. Your aunt informed me that she will be accompanied by her son Thomas. She wishes you to accommodate him for three days.'

'Young Thos! I would prefer not to touch him with the proverbial tenfoot pole, Jeeves; he is a youth totally unfit for human consumption even on the emptiest of stomachs. Doubtless Aunt Agatha wants him to be shunted round dentists and Old Vics and things before leaving for his school at Bramley-on-Sea.'

'Precisely, sir. It is not an inviting prospect.'

'Still, Jeeves, we must remember that in this life it is not aunts that matter but the courage one brings to dealing with them.'

'A commendably stoic attitude, sir, but, if I may say so, one hard to sustain without refreshment of a special sort. I have prepared a Churchill for you.' I drank deep and ceased to quiver from brilliantine to shoesole.

'There goes the bell, Jeeves. Unleash these horrors. I feel strong and resolute. I shall not gratify the whims of this aunt.'

BRANDY FIX

1 measure brandy
½ measure cherry brandy
1 teaspoon of sugar
Juice of one lemon
Slice of lemon

Dissolve sugar in a little water in an old-fashioned glass. Put in the other ingredients, top up with crushed ice. Add slice of lemon and stir. Serve with straws.

BRANDY FLIP

1 measure brandy
1 whole egg
1 teaspoon of sugar
Grated nutmeg on top

Shake well and strain into a wine glass. Top with grated nutmeg.

BRANDY COCKTAIL

⅘ brandy
⅕ sweet vermouth
Dash of angostura bitters

Stir and strain into a cocktail glass.

CHURCHILL

⅓ Calvados or Applejack
⅔ yellow Chartreuse

Shake well and strain into a cocktail glass.

GLOOM CHASER

$\frac{1}{4}$ Grand Marnier
$\frac{1}{4}$ white curaçao
$\frac{1}{4}$ Grenadine
$\frac{1}{4}$ lemon juice

Shake and strain into a cocktail glass.

GROG

1 measure dark rum
1 lump of sugar
2 cloves
Dash of lemon juice
Small stick of cinnamon
Boiling water to top up

Put in an old-fashioned glass and stir.

HAMLET

$\frac{1}{3}$ Tuaca
$\frac{1}{3}$ white crème de menthe
$\frac{1}{3}$ cream

Shake well and strain into a wine glass.

HANDLEBAR

1 measure Scotch
$\frac{1}{2}$ measure Drambuie
$\frac{1}{3}$ measure lime cordial

Shake and strain into a cocktail glass.

IRISH COFFEE

1 measure Irish whiskey
Hot strong coffee
2 teaspoons Demarara sugar
Cream

Stir whiskey and sugar in a wine glass of hot coffee.
Float cream on top by pouring over the back of a warm spoon.
Do not stir.

HOT TODDY

1 measure Scotch (rum, gin or any whisky)
1 teaspoon of sugar
2 cloves
1 slice of lemon
1 stick of cinnamon (optional)
Boiling water to top up

Put all ingredients in an old-fashioned glass, topping up with the hot water. Stir.

HOT BUTTERED RUM

1 measure dark rum
1 lump of sugar
Slither of butter
4 cloves
Cinnamon stick (optional)
Boiling water to top up

Put all ingredients in an old-fashioned glass and stir.

REBEL

$\frac{2}{3}$ bourbon
$\frac{1}{3}$ crème de menthe
Dash of Calvados or Applejack

Shake well and strain into a cocktail glass over ice.

ROBIN HOOD

$\frac{2}{3}$ Scotch
$\frac{1}{3}$ Lillet

Stir well and strain into a cocktail glass.

RUSTY NAIL

$\frac{1}{3}$ Drambuie
$\frac{2}{3}$ Scotch
Twist of lemon peel (optional)

Serve 'on the rocks' in an old-fashioned glass. Add lemon peel.

SAZERAC

$\frac{3}{4}$ rye
$\frac{1}{4}$ sugar syrup
Dash of angostura bitters
Dash of pastis
Twist of lemon peel

Stir and strain into a cocktail glass.

SIDECAR

$\frac{1}{2}$ brandy
$\frac{1}{4}$ Cointreau
$\frac{1}{4}$ lemon juice

Shake and strain into a cocktail glass.

TODDY

1 measure Scotch (rum, gin, or any whisky)
1 teaspoon of sugar

Dissolve sugar in a little water in an old-fashioned glass
Add spirit and ice and stir.

GOOD OLD SUMMERTIME

'A perfect day, Jeeves. What's that thing of yours about larks?'

'Sir?'

'And, I rather think, snails.'

'"The lark's on the wing, the snail's on the thorn. . ."'

'That's it. And the punchline?'

'"God's in his heaven—All's right with the world."'

'Thank you, Jeeves. It is in this very garden that I have got engaged three times. No business resulted, but the fact remains. These romantic surroundings go straight to the head. Great lovers through the ages have probably fixed up the preliminary formalities on this very spot. The place is simply stiff with atmosphere. You stroll with a girl in the shady walks. You sit with her on sun-dappled lawns. Plant anyone here and, in a trice, he will be reaching out for the nearest girl and slapping his soul down in front of her. . . .'

Jeeves gave one of his admonitory coughs, and I turned to see a girl more like Clara Bow than anything human. My soul was instantly prostrate at her feet. Meanwhile my empty frame, abandoned in a deckchair, whispered urgent instructions in the right quarter. 'Jeeves, mix a brace of love potions. There is man's work to be done.'

APPLE COCKTAIL

1 oz sweet cider
$\frac{1}{2}$ oz dry gin
$\frac{1}{2}$ oz brandy
1 oz Calvados or Applejack

Shake well and strain into a cocktail glass.

AUTUMN GOLD

1 measure mandarine liqueur
Vintage cider to top up
Mint leaf, slice of orange, cherry to decorate

Put cracked ice in a highball glass. Add mandarine liqueur and top up with the cider. Decorate with mint leaf and fruit.

BUCK'S FIZZ

Iced champagne
Juice of one orange

Put orange juice in a wine glass and fill it with champagne.

CHOCOLATE COCKTAIL

1 measure vodka
1 measure white crème de menthe
1 scoop chocolate ice cream

Blend well and serve in a highball glass.

COBBLER

1 measure gin (rum, brandy or whisky)

4 dashes orange curaçao

1 teaspoon of sugar

Fruit to decorate

Sprig of mint (optional)

Serve on the rocks in a wine glass, stir and decorate with fruit.
Serve with straws.

CUBA LIBRE

1 measure white rum

Juice and rind of half a lime (or lemon)

Coca Cola

Extract juice from lime (lemon) and put both rind and juice in a
highball glass with the rum and ice. Top up with Coca Cola and
stir. Serve with straws.

FRENCH '75

1 measure gin

$\frac{1}{4}$ measure fresh lemon juice

1 teaspoon sugar syrup

Few dashes of egg white

Champagne to top up

Shake well. Strain into a champagne glass and float the
champagne on top. Can also be made in large quantities
in a punch bowl.

GUISEPPE'S SPECIAL

2 measures apricot brandy

$\frac{1}{2}$ measure orange juice

$\frac{1}{2}$ measure pineapple juice

1 scoop of pistachio ice cream

Blend and serve in a highball glass.

MOSCOW MULE

1 measure vodka

Ginger beer to top up

Juice of one lemon (or lime)

Sprigs of mint to decorate

Put ingredients in a highball glass with ice.
Decorate with mint and serve with straws.

PALM COURT DELIGHT

$\frac{2}{3}$ ice-cold champagne

$\frac{1}{3}$ fresh orange juice

Grand Marnier

Put champagne and orange juice in a champagne glass.
Add few dashes of Grand Marnier and stir.

PIMM'S

1 measure Pimm's

Lemonade to top up

Slice of lemon

Slither of cucumber

Mint leaves

Pour over ice in a highball glass.
Decorate with lemon, cucumber and mint.

PINA COLADA

$2\frac{1}{2}$ oz pineapple juice

$1\frac{1}{2}$ oz Bacardi rum

1 oz cream of coconut

Dash of Cointreau

Half a cup of crushed ice

Blend all ingredients together for 2–3 minutes and serve
unstrained in a highball glass.

PINEAPPLE RUMRUNNER

1 large pineapple
1 measure Bacardi rum
$\frac{1}{2}$ measure apricot brandy
$\frac{1}{2}$ measure fresh pineapple juice
$\frac{1}{2}$ measure orange juice
$\frac{1}{2}$ measure lemon juice
$\frac{1}{4}$ measure Grenadine

Fruit to garnish pineapple e.g. cherries, pineapple chunks, orange slices. Cut the top off the pineapple and scoop out the flesh. Put pineapple flesh and other cocktail ingredients into a blender with crushed ice. Return blended cocktail to the hollow pineapple and cut small hole in the 'lid' so that the drink can be sucked out by straw. Garnish a face on the pineapple using any suitable fruit.

PLANTERS PUNCH

1 measure dark rum
1 teaspoon of Grenadine
Dash of angostura bitters
$\frac{1}{2}$ measure fresh lime (or lemon) juice
Soda water to top up
Slices of orange and lemon to decorate

Fill a highball glass with crushed ice. Put ingredients in glass and stir. Decorate with orange and lemon and serve with straws.

43

SANGRIA

3 pints red burgundy
1 bottle champagne or soda water
2 measures brandy
½ measure Cointreau
Juice of one lemon
Assorted fruit—one sliced orange and lemon
Bananas, apples and grapes (without skin or pips)

Let mixture stand for two or three hours to allow flavours of the fruits to be thoroughly absorbed. Serve well iced.

SNAPDRAGON

2 measures vodka
1 measure crème de menthe
Soda water to top up

Pour into highball glass over ice and top up with soda water. Stir.

SNOWBALL

1 measure advocaat
Dash of lime cordial
Lemonade to top up
Slice of orange
Maraschino cherry

Serve in highball glass over ice, top up with lemonade and decorate with fruit. Serve with straws.

SOUTH SIDE

1 measure vodka
Juice of one lemon
1 teaspoon of sugar
Fresh mint leaves to decorate

Shake well and strain into a champagne glass over cracked ice. Decorate with mint. Serve with straws.

SUNRISE

2 parts tequila

1 part Galliano

1 part crème de banane

1 part cream

Few drops of Grenadine

Dash of lemon juice

Shake and strain into a cocktail glass.

TEQUILA SUNRISE

1 part tequila

4 parts fresh orange juice

Few dashes of Grenadine

Serve tequila and orange juice 'on the rocks' in a highball glass and float the Grenadine on the top so that the drink is given a streaky effect.

WRANGLER

1 measure vodka

Dash of Benedictine

2 measures apple juice

Juice of half an orange

Dash of egg white

Shake and strain into a champagne glass.

YELLOW LILY

$\frac{1}{2}$ Bacardi rum

$\frac{1}{4}$ amaretto

$\frac{1}{4}$ fresh orange juice

Shake and strain into a cocktail glass.

WING DING RAN DAN

'Ever tried tossing a card into a hat, Jeeves?'

'No sir. But I am aware of the diversion.'

'Well, this morning, the Drones team of card-throwers took on the Lizard's Club and bally well lost.'

'I trust this sporting failure has not occasioned any marked distress among the members, sir?'

'You trust in vain, Jeeves. The club's repute is in tatters. Fortunes have changed hands. Standing room only for aching hearts.'

'Luncheon in no way restored the young gentlemen's spirits, sir?'

'No Jeeves. Effervescence was conspicuous by its ab. The whole thing was more like Christmas dinner on Devil's Island.'

'May I put forward a proposition, sir?'

'Propose away, Jeeves.'

The poet Housman, sir, says "He that drinks in season, shall live before he dies."'

'Are you suggesting a spree or binge by way of consolation?'

'Yes, sir.'

'So that our troubles may vanish like dew on the what's-it? You have delivered the goods, Jeeves.

Summon the finest and fairest in the land to the Wooster home this very night. Let the bowl flow with Rum Punch, Royal Silver and Sherry Sangaree. . .'

'With pleasure, sir, but may I suggest not all at the same time? The mélange might not be entirely satisfactory.'

'Your attention to detail, Jeeves, is untiring. What did the fellow say about those fellows beating it up on a boat?'

'"Youth on the prow, and Pleasure at the helm . . ."'

'These poets put their fingers on the nub, Jeeves, what?'

'So I have always been disposed to believe, sir.'

MRS. BURCH'S EGG NOGG

1 quart bourbon
13 eggs
13 tablespoons of sugar
1 quart whipping cream

Beat yolk of eggs with sugar until white. Add whisky very, very slowly, stirring constantly. Let mixture set overnight or for several hours as the bourbon 'cooks' the eggs and it will not separate later. When ready to serve, whip the cream and beat egg whites. Add cream slowly to mixture and fold in the egg whites. This makes about $\frac{3}{4}$ of a gallon. Serve with spoons.

FISH HOUSE PUNCH

$\frac{1}{4}$ pint peach brandy
$\frac{1}{4}$ pint dark rum
$\frac{1}{2}$ pint brandy
1 cup of sugar
Juice of 6 lemons
3 pints sparkling mineral water

Stir mixture thoroughly and pour into a punch bowl over ice. Makes about 14 cups.

HOT CIDER PUNCH

2 pints sweet cider
$\frac{1}{4}$ pint water
4 tablespoons of sugar
4 cloves
1 large orange
1 teaspoon of allspice
$\frac{1}{2}$–1 teaspoon of powdered ginger
Grated nutmeg

Press cloves into the orange and bake it in a moderate oven to bring out the flavour. Pare rinds from the lemons and simmer in water for about 10 minutes. Strain and add sugar to the liquid. Return to the pan with the lemon juice, spices and cider. Bring mixture to the boil. Slice the baked orange into a punch bowl and pour the boiling cider mixture over it. Top with grated nutmeg. Makes about 8 cups.

MULLED ALE

2 pints ale

1 measure rum or brandy

1 tablespoon of sugar

Pinch of ground cloves

Pinch of powdered ginger

Heat all the ingredients together in a pan.
Serve in a warm punch bowl. Makes about 8 cups.

MULLED WINE

1 bottle red wine

1 wine glass of port

$\frac{1}{4}$ pint of water

1 tablespoon of sugar

Thinly sliced rind of half a lemon and/or a stick of cinnamon

12 whole cloves

Pinch of grated nutmeg

Put spices in the water and simmer in a pan for half an hour.
Strain through a sieve and pour the wine into the pan, adding the
spiced water to this. Add port and sugar and bring mixture to the
boil. Serve very hot with thin slices of lemon peel and/or the
cinnamon stick. Makes about 8 glasses.

NEGUS

1 bottle sherry

1 quart boiling water

1 lemon

1 measure brandy

Nutmeg

Sugar

Warm sherry very gently in a saucepan, add sliced lemon and
pour in boiling water. Add a little nutmeg and sugar to taste and
finally the brandy. Makes about 12 glasses.

ROYAL SILVER

$\frac{1}{2}$ fresh grapefruit juice
$\frac{1}{4}$ eau de vie de poire William
$\frac{1}{4}$ Cointreau
Champagne to top up
Sugar

Moisten rim of a champagne glass and dip it in the sugar. Shake and strain cocktail into the glass and top up with champagne.

RUM PUNCH

1 bottle rum
1 bottle brandy
Juice of 9 lemons
12 teaspoons powdered sugar
Soda water to taste
Fruit to decorate

Place ingredients in a punch bowl with a block of ice and decorate with slices of fruit in season. Keep stirring. Makes about 12 cups.

SHERRY SANGAREE

1 measure sherry (or port)
1 teaspoon of sugar
Slice of lemon
Grated nutmeg

Fill an old-fashioned glass with crushed ice, add ingredients and top with the nutmeg. Stir and serve with straws.

SYLLABUB

1 measure sweet sherry

$\frac{1}{2}$ measure whipping cream

$\frac{1}{2}$ measure milk

1 teaspoon fine sugar

Beat all ingredients together and serve in a champagne glass.
To be eaten with a teaspoon.

CORPSE REVIVERS

In my end is my beginning as the fellow said. I began by telling you about those pick-me-ups of Jeeves and their effect on a fellow who is hanging on to life by a thread the morning after; and I conclude in the same vein. It has been well said of Bertram Wooster that if he has been on a bender he will not palter with the truth the morning after. He will be the first to admit that he has been out on the tiles; outstepping Fred, most nimble of all the Astaires, at the place of the moment; squiring girls with oomph and all the fixings. And, it has to be added, mopping the stuff up like a vacuum-cleaner until it laps against the tonsils.

Normally the Wooster ration is fairly circumspect but, when celebrating or under stress, more than a touch more finds its way down the hatch and, once back at the Wooster residence, I often further illuminate an already brilliantly lit interior.

I wake, ganglions vibrating, and see, through a heavy mist, Jeeves at my side all set to ease the young master back into mid-season form.

'The vital essence, Jeeves?'

'You are kind enough to describe it as such, sir.'

I then swallow and, for perhaps part of a split second, nothing happens. It is as though all nature waits breathless. Then, suddenly, it is as if the Last Trump had been played on Judgement Day. Bonfires burst out in all parts of the frame, a steam hammer strikes the back of the head, ears ring loudly, eyeballs rotate and there is a tingling about the brow.

Then matters clarify. The smoke clears. The ears cease to ring. Birds twitter. The sun comes up with a jerk and, a moment later, all is peace, sweetness and light.

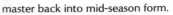

BLACK VELVET

½ chilled Guinness

½ chilled dry champagne

Serve in a beer mug or tankard without ice.

BLOODY MARY

1 measure vodka

Tomato juice to top up

Few dashes Worcester sauce

A little lemon juice

Salt and pepper

Dash of Tabasco

Put vodka in a highball or old-fashioned glass over ice. Add
Worcester sauce, tabasco, lemon juice and seasoning and top up
with tomato juice. Stir. (This drink can also be shaken and
strained)

BULL SHOT

1 measure vodka

2 measures consommé or beef bouillon

Dash of Worcestershire sauce

Dash of lemon juice

Dash of celery salt

Dash of cayenne pepper

Dash of Tabasco

Shake and strain into an old-fashioned glass.

CAIPIRINHA

| 2 measures vodka or white rum |
| 1 whole lime, quartered |
| Sugar |
| Crushed ice |

Put quartered lime in an old-fashioned glass and add enough sugar to thoroughly coat the fruit. Mash lime and sugar together with a spoon and add vodka and crushed ice.

CORPSE REVIVER

| $\frac{1}{3}$ sweet vermouth |
| $\frac{1}{3}$ Calvados |
| $\frac{1}{3}$ brandy |

Stir and strain into a cocktail glass.

HAIR OF THE DOG

| $\frac{1}{2}$ measure Scotch |
| 1 measure thick cream |
| $\frac{1}{2}$ measure honey |

Shake well with shaved ice and strain into a cocktail glass.

HARRY'S PICK ME UP

| 1 measure brandy |
| 1 teaspoon of Grenadine |
| Juice of half a lemon |
| Champagne to top up |

Shake well and strain into a wine glass. Top up with champagne.

MILK PUNCH

| 1 measure whisky or rum |
| 1 glass of milk |
| 1 tablespoon of sugar |
| Grated nutmeg to top |

Shake well and strain into a highball glass. Top with grated nutmeg.

MORNING MASHIE

| $\frac{1}{2}$ gin |
| $\frac{1}{2}$ lemon juice |
| Few dashes of pastis |
| Dash of anisette |
| Dash of angostura bitters |
| Dash of egg white |

Shake and strain into a wine glass.

PICK ME UP

| 1 measure brandy |
| $\frac{1}{4}$ pint of milk |
| Dash of angostura bitters |
| 1 teaspoon of sugar |
| Soda to top up |

Shake and strain into a highball glass. Top up with soda.

PRAIRIE OYSTER

| Yolk of an egg (unbroken) |
| 1 teaspoon Worcestershire sauce |
| 1 teaspoon tomato sauce |
| 2 dashes of vinegar |
| Dash of pepper |

Drink this from a wine glass.

RITZ REVIVER

$\frac{2}{3}$ Fernet-Branca

$\frac{1}{3}$ crème de menthe

Dash of angostura bitters

Piece of orange peel

Rub rim of a cocktail glass with the orange peel.
Shake and strain cocktail into glass and drop in orange peel.

SAVOY CORPSE REVIVER

$\frac{1}{3}$ white crème de menthe

$\frac{1}{3}$ Fernet-Branca

$\frac{1}{3}$ brandy

Shake and strain into a cocktail glass.

THE SUFFERING BASTARD

$\frac{1}{2}$ measure gin

$\frac{1}{2}$ measure brandy

Few dashes of angostura bitters

1 teaspoon of lime juice cordial

Cold ginger ale to top up

Slices of lime, cucumber and orange to decorate

Sprig of mint

Swirl angostura bitters around a highball glass and toss off the
excess. Half fill the glass with ice and add the gin, brandy, lime
juice and the ginger ale. Decorate with slices of fruit
and sprig of mint.

INDEX

Many of the recipes are
printed by kind
permission of the
bartenders at the following
places:

Boodle's Club
Boodle's Cocktail
Boodle's Original
Snapdragon

21 Club, New York
Et tu Brute
Oh Henry
Green Monkey
King George VI
Matador
Hamlet
Churchill
Rebel
South Side
Jezebel

Quaglino's
Tantalizer
Lifter
Leaper
Wrangler

Savoy Hotel
'76
Happy Return
Yellow Lily
Savoy Corpse Reviver
Royal Silver

Langan's Brasserie
Mandarine Royale
French '75

Hotel Bristol
Everton Blue
Morning Mashie

Peppermint Park
Hong Kong Gin Fizz
Guiseppe's Special
Chocolate Cocktail

Bas and Annie's
Pineapple Rumrunner
Chop Nut

Ritz Hotel
Ritz Reviver
Palm Court Delight

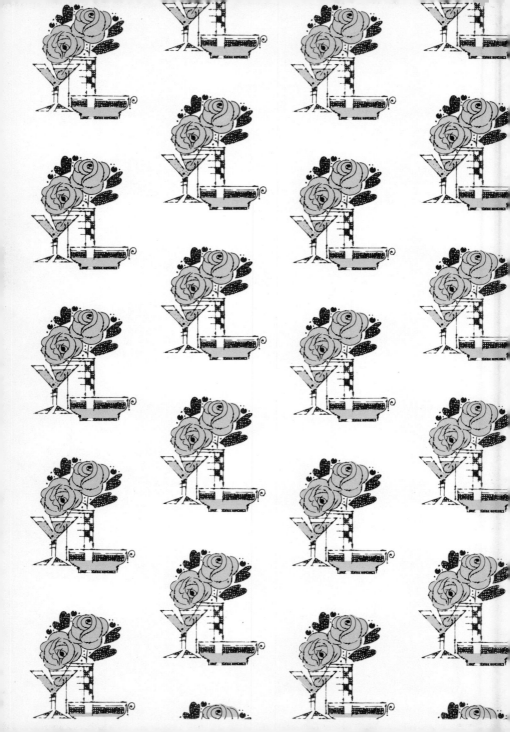